Living Bread

Donald Hilton

NATIONAL CHRISTIAN EDUCATION COUNCIL

Other worship resources published by NCEC

Celebrating Series . . .
A series of six books for all-age festival services:
Celebrating Christmas Books 1 & 2
Celebrating Lent & Easter Books 1 & 2
Celebrating Harvest
Celebrating Special Sundays

Anthologies of material for private reflection and public worship
A Word in Season
Liturgy of Life
Prayers for the Church Community

Cover design: Julian Smith
Cover photo: Ffotograff, Cardiff

Published by:
National Christian Education Council
Robert Denholm House
Nutfield
Redhill, RH1 4HW

British Library Cataloguing-in-Publication Data:
Hilton, Donald
    Living Bread – (Living Worship Series)
    I. Title II. Series
    264

ISBN 0-7197-0807-9

First published 1993
© 1993 Donald Hilton

Typeset by Avonset, Midsomer Norton, Bath
Printed in Great Britain by
Clifford Frost Ltd., Wimbledon, London

CONTENTS

FOREWORD TO THE SERIES

This is the third in a series of six books which offer services of worship for all ages in the church. The details of the other five can be found on the back cover of the book. The authors write from a wide experience of leading all-age worship and the *Living Worship series* . . . springs from that experience.

In the celebration of Christian worship every age-group has something to contribute. The experiences of each member of the congregation, regardless of age, can be used, and should be valued. The ability and willingness of children to enter into a wide range of worship experiences should not be under-estimated. Adults should be encouraged to accept the gifts which children bring to worship.

There is no 'audience' in all-age worship. The children are not performing for the adults; neither are they passive spectators to adult worship. These services provide the means by which the whole church family can engage in its most important responsibility and joy: the worship of God through Jesus Christ.

These books will serve churches best when a group of people, representative of all ages in the church meet to plan the worship, and are prepared to give time and thought to the preparation. Those who use them should feel free to adapt them to the needs of the local church community. In any one church they may well emerge on a Sunday morning looking quite different from the details given on the printed pages that follow.

Unless the flow of the service requires it, no place is given for either the Lord's Prayer, the offertory, or announcements. These should be included according to local practice.

Series Editor: Donald Hilton

PREFACE

Children are increasingly being recognised as integral to the local church rather than only potential members of the community of faith. One consequence is that in a growing number of churches they are welcomed to the Lord's Supper, receiving the bread and wine.

When their presence is taken seriously adult members of the church often find that new light is thrown on their own participation in the Communion Service. These four services have grown out of that conviction and experience, and have been written in the hope that, whilst sharing in the Communion Service, children and others will also learn more of its meaning, especially if the service, is new to them.

These services follow the basic liturgical pattern of the communion service, though not slavishly. They seek to express the ideas of the service in a way that all except the very youngest children can understand. Children will not fully understand all that the Lord's Supper signifies – but that is true of adults as well. It is a service into which we grow, and which grows with us.

This book contains four services. Each one focuses on one element of the service i.e. thanksgiving, remembrance, the service as a celebration feast, and personal and community renewal.

Worship leaders should have access to the usual books of Communion services and supplement what is offered here where this is suggested.

Donald Hilton

THANK GOD!

Introduction

Thanksgiving is an essential element within the Communion Service. This festival service begins by calling on everyday experiences for which people want to thank God, moves on to our thanksgiving for the gift of Christ, and then sets both within the Communion Service.

Preparation

Invite church-members of mixed ages to meet and decide how they can best express a sense of thanksgiving for the ordinary things of life. Talk about their own experiences of life. Give them newspapers or magazines, items from which might prompt their gratitude. Plan the groups so that each one uses a different method to express thanksgiving e.g., write prayers of thanksgiving, write a poem on 'the happiest day of my life', prepare a dance sequence on the theme of thanksgiving, show a selection of transparencies to inspire gratitude, make a collage of pictures cut from magazines etc. Many groups will have other ideas about how to communicate a sense of gratitude.

ORDER OF SERVICE

Call to worship

Let the Holy Spirit fill you: speak to one another in psalms, hymns and songs; sing and make music from your heart to the Lord; and in the name of our Lord Jesus Christ give thanks every day for everything to our God and Father

Ephesians 5.18b-20 (REB)

Prayer of Confession

Heavenly Father, we want to approach you with thanksgiving for all that you have given us, and praise for who you are, yet we must begin with sorrow and sadness.
We are sorry that so often we spoil the gifts you give,
or hoard them selfishly,
or forget who it is that has given them.

7

Knowing our foolishness and sin we pray that today our thanksgiving will be genuine and heartfelt, and that through your forgiving love, we shall be led to live the kind of life you always intended for us.

Hymn   'Thank you for giving me this morning'
            or another hymn expressing gratitude

Thanks a million
Invite the groups who prepared their ways of expressing gratitude to come forward and share their ideas. The worship leader will need to consult with the group-leaders in advance so as to link the work of the various groups together effectively.

Prayer
Thank you, Lord, thank you.
Thank you for all the gifts you have given me today.
Thank you for all I have seen, heard, received.
Thank you for the water that woke me up,
     the soap that smells good,
     the toothpaste that refreshes.
Thank you for the clothes that protect me, for their colour and style.
Thank you for the newspapers so faithfully there, for the comics, my morning smile, for useful meetings, for justice done and big games won.
Thank you for my work, my tools, my efforts.

Thank you for the food that sustained me, the drink that refreshed me.
Thank you for the boy I watched playing on the footpath opposite.
Thank you for his skate board and for his comical face when he fell.

Thank you for the morning greetings we received, and all the smiles from those at home and church,
for tactful affection and silent presence.
Thank you for the roof that shelters me, for the lamp that lights me, for the radio that plays, for the news, for music and singing.
Thank you for the flowers, so pretty on the table.
Thank you for the bread and the wine, already prepared.

Thank you for the tranquil night.
Thank you for the stars.
Thank you for the silence.

Thank you for the time you have given me.
Thank you for life.
Thank you for grace.

Thank you for being there, Lord.
Thank you for listening to me, for taking me seriously, for
gathering my gifts in your hands to offer them to the Father.
Thank you, Lord.
Thank you.

Michel Quoist

Hymn   'O Lord of heaven and earth and sea'
or 'For air and sunshine'

*Either distribute paper to the congregation and invite them to write, in not
more than 15 words, something for which they want to say 'thank you' to
God. Collect the papers and invite one or more people to take them into
another room and produce a prayer from them which will be used as part of
the eucharistic (thanksgiving) prayer later in the service.*
    *Or invite people to call out the things for which they want to give thanks.
Make a note of these and base the later prayer on your notes.*

Readings
*Select some of the following readings. Choose a different reader for each one
you select.*
    In the beginning God made the world.
    Let us give thanks for all that God has made.

    Think of a time when you saw that the world is beautiful . . .
    Think of a sunset over the hills,
        or sunrise over a sleeping city.
    Think of a running river,
        or stars shining on a dark sea.
    Think of lights flashing on a puddle,
        or of geraniums growing in a window box.
    Think of an time when you saw that the world is beautiful
        – and give thanks.

Think of a time when you found pleasure in your body . . .
think of walking in the wind, or digging the garden.
Think of dancing till dawn, or climbing a mountain.
Think of giving birth to a child,
    or holding someone you love.
Think of a time when you found pleasure in your body
    – and give thanks.

Iona Community

Psalm 116.5-14

Romans 7.21-25 or 1 Corinthians 15.50-57 or 2 Corinthians 9.8-15
or other Biblical reading which gives thanks to God for Jesus
Christ.

Glory to God in the highest,
and peace to his people on earth.
Lord God, heavenly King
almighty God and Father,
we worship you, we give you thanks,
we praise you for your glory.
Lord Jesus Christ, only Son of the Father,
Lord God, Lamb of God,
you take away the sin of the world:
have mercy on us;
you are seated at the right hand of the Father:
receive our prayer.
For you alone are the Holy One,
you alone are the Lord,
you alone are the Most High,
Jesus Christ, with the Holy Spirit,
in the glory of God the Father. Amen

Offering of money
Introduce as a way of giving thanks for all that God has given us.

Comment
Saying thank you is a natural human response. It is a mark of being
human. It is our response to the gift of life and creation around us.
The ungrateful have lost a part of their humanity.

Christians have special cause to be grateful. First, because we not
only receive the gifts of creation like everyone else but also because

we know the God from whom they come. Secondly, God's gifts to us have been crowned by the gift of Christ's life and teaching.

When Douglas Hyde was converted from communism to Christianity he said, 'Now, at last I have someone to whom I can say "thank you" '. Believers have always felt that way. To be able to respond to a gift is itself part of the joy of receiving. Thanksgiving is a response Christians put at the heart of the Communion Service. Indeed, some Christians call the service, 'the Eucharist' which is the Greek word that means 'thanksgiving'.

Table preparation

Continue to introduce the service with the following comments as the table is prepared. Use people of different ages to assist in the preparation. Do not be afraid of short periods of silence as people move to and from the table with the various items.

Just as at home, first, a table-cloth is laid across the table. Ours is pure white; a sign that this is a special meal. (*The cloth is carefully laid across the table*)

Now the money we have already given is placed on the table. We gave the money to show our gratitude for everything God has given to us. (*The money is put on the table*)

Earlier in the service we each wrote down those things for which we have special cause to say thank you to God. They will soon become our prayer of thanksgiving. Now they are on a plate and are laid on the table; sign of our thanksgiving. (*Those who have prepared the eucharistic prayer lay the papers on a plate on the table*)

And now the bread; a token of all the food we eat. 'Give us this day our daily bread', we pray, and he does. In loving intercession we remember those in the world who are hungry. They also pray for their daily bread and God is asking us to make their prayers come true. But this bread is not only a symbol of our daily bread; it is a sign of Jesus Christ who loved us so much that he was willing to give himself, and die on the cross. During the Last Supper, when this Communion Service was first held, Jesus took bread, and having said a blessing he broke it and gave it to the disciples with the words:

'Take this and eat; this is my body.' (*The plate of bread is laid on the table*)

And the wine. (*The wine is placed on the table*) As the bread reminded us of all the food that a loving God gives us so this wine reminds us of the all refreshing drink. At the Last Supper Jesus gave the wine a new meaning. Listen to what he did and said:

'Then he took a cup, and having offered thanks to God he gave it to them with the words: "Drink from it, all of you. For this is my blood, the blood of the covenant, shed for many for the forgiveness of sins." '

And finally, the cross. (*The cross is placed on the table*) The cross helps us to understand the meaning of it all. He must have loved us greatly to give his life. Now we know just how much God loves all his creation and loves us, his people.

Hymn of thanksgiving for Jesus Christ
e.g. 'Lord Jesus Christ, you have come to us'
'Jesus the Lord says, "I am the bread" '

Prayers of thanksgiving.
First use the prayer compiled from the personal thanksgivings the congregation wrote down. It could become a responsive prayer, the leader saying:
For this we give you thanks, eternal God

And the people replying:
You deserve the thankful praise of all your people.

Then use the following prayer:
Holy, holy, holy Lord.
God of power and might,
Heaven and earth are full of your glory.
Hosanna in the highest.
Lord Jesus Christ, we believe that you are always present with your people. You are with us now, invisible but very real. We thank you for all you said, all you did and the way you still speak to us and act for us.
As in this church we do what you did in the upstairs room so long ago, we pray that the Holy Spirit will help us to understand.
As our daily bread at home makes us strong in our bodies to work and play, so may this bread give us spiritual strength.
As our drinking, day by day, refreshes us and quenches our thirst, may this wine refresh us in our spirits.
Receiving this food and drink may we find spiritual health and strength so that we can truly be your people working, loving, and serving in your world, until your Kingdom comes.

Additional traditional prayers may be used.

The breaking and sharing of the bread.

The sharing of the wine.

Prayer
Father God, we will always thank you because you are always
good to us.
We will always praise you because you always deserve it.
We will serve you as long as we live because we are your people.
We are your friends because you first befriended us.
We will serve others with joy because that is how your people
act. Amen

Hymn   'Here, Lord, we take the broken bread'
          or 'Be known to us in breaking bread'

Benediction

I REMEMBER IT WELL

Introduction

'Do this in memory of me', Jesus said at the Last Supper. Thus, amongst other things, the Communion Service is a memorial to Christ and evokes the long memory of the Church. Every Christian congregation contributes to this memory. Some older people in your congregation will remember church services and other events of sixty or more years ago, and also recall their grandparents telling of events sixty years before that. Children have a shorter memory but those who remember 'what we did last Christmas' or 'what fun we had on the church family outing even though it rained' are all contributing to that vast reservoir of memory which is a major resource in the Church. This service calls on that local memory, uses the long memory of the Church's centuries as a further resource, and celebrates the meal which being embedded in the memory of the Church, has become a source of spiritual strength and affirmation.

Preparation

Several interviews are suggested within this service. Choose the people carefully and make the appropriate arrangements.

Paper and a quill pen are needed at a table off-centre from the communion table. Bread, wine, and a white cloth should be prepared in advance.

ORDER OF SERVICE

Call to worship

The church – every gathering of the church, everywhere, under every form – remembers that on a certain night its Founder said and did certain things, briefly reported; that on the same night he fell into the hands of his enemies; and that he suffered a violent death. All lines run back to that precise point, which we might tentatively date Friday April 7th, AD 30.

The remembrance goes back in a continuous chain. At every service there are present elderly people who, fifty or sixty years

14

ago heard those words spoken by, or in the presence of, men old enough to be their grandparents; there are young people who, it may be, will repeat them in the hearing of their grandchildren. And so the endless chain goes on. For nineteen centuries there has not been one single week in which this act of remembrance was not made, one generation reminding another.

C.H. Dodd

C.H. Dodd, a well-known Biblical scholar wrote those words. This morning, as we come to a Communion Service, we will form one more link in that chain and ourselves both share in, and add to, the long memory of the Church.

Hymn   'To Abraham and Sarah'
              or 'Christ is the King! O friends rejoice'

Introduction
How long is the memory of the congregation about their own local church. Ask the people to raise their hands if they have known the church for five years? . . . ten? . . . twenty? . . . thirty? . . . fifty? And this is only one church. Many will remember three, four, or more local churches as they have moved around the country or the world.

Are there families in the church whose corporate memory goes back through parents, grandparents, great-grandparents, or even longer?

Interviews
Interview two or three individual people or groups of people about their memory of events in your own church. It is important to use some of the older members of the church who may remember some important events such as the induction of a well-known minister, the opening of new buildings, the war-time Sunday the air raid warning went and the service was finished in the shelter, or more personal events such as how the church showed its care to someone in hospital.

Do not ignore the value of children's memory as they recall last Christmas or a special anniversary. If a meal was part of any of the memories make the point that it is natural for people to celebrate by eating together. Briefly comment on this for birthdays, Christmas, anniversaries etc.

Leader
But the Church's memory is much longer than one church! The corporate memory of the world-wide Church of Jesus Christ covers the

overflowing churches of the Victorian age in Britain, and the struggle of eastern European churches under communism. The Pilgrim Fathers setting sail for America to avoid persecution in Britain, the day Martin Luther nailed his manifesto to the cathedral door in Wittenberg, the moment when Francis of Assisi heard the call to poverty and service, and the times when Mother Julian of Norwich received her visions are all part of our church's memory this morning. Whitfield and Wesley share our worship with us, as does Martin Luther King, Mother Teresa, Augustine, Columba, Benedict, Joan of Arc, and countless others. Hymns and prayers refresh our memory about much of our history, and the Bible takes us right to the beginning of our Christian faith. Peter and Paul, James and John, the centurion's servant, Mary and Martha, Prisca and Aquila, and the widow of Nain are all part of the long flowing tide of Christian memory.

Some of the above names can be changed in the light of the local church's own tradition.

Hymn

Select a hymn which reflects the history of the Church. The following are suggestions.

'Jesus our mighty Lord' (*Clement of Alexandria; 2nd century*)
'Hail, gladdening light' (*Greek 4th century*)
'Let all mortal flesh keep silence' (*From Liturgy of St. James; 4th century*)

Prayer

As we share this prayer of confession and hope we use words written about 1200 years ago.

Eternal Light, shine into our hearts,
Eternal Goodness, deliver us from evil,
Eternal Power, be our support,
Eternal Wisdom, scatter the darkness of our ignorance,
Eternal Pity, have mercy on us;
that with all our heart and mind and soul and strength we may seek thy face and be brought by thine infinite mercy to thy holy presence; through Jesus Christ our Lord. Amen

Alcuin (735-804)

Leader

At the heart of the memory of the Church is the celebration of the Lord's Supper. Dom Gregory Dix reminds us how often and in what countless circumstances it has been celebrated.

'Do this in memory of me', Jesus said as he broke bread and shared wine.

Was ever another command so obeyed? For century after century, spreading slowly to every continent and country and among every race on earth, this action has been done, in every conceivable human circumstance, for every conceivable human need from infancy and before it to extreme old-age and after it, from pinnacles of earthly greatness to the refuge of fugitives in the caves and dens of the earth.

Dom Gregory Dix

Invite one, or perhaps two people to speak very briefly on a particular Communion Service they recall.

Leader

Listen to these stories. They tell us of some Communion services that, through the memory of the world-wide Church of Jesus Christ now belong to us all. Our sharing of bread and wine this morning will become another story in that long and continuing tradition.

Readings

1. *Christmas in prison*

It is Christmas-time, but Christmas in the dark days of the war with Nazi Germany. Hanns Lilje, a minister, was a prisoner of the Gestapo. He tells us what happened one Christmas Eve.

'I was walking up and down my cell, looking at a nativity scene which one if my children had made for me; illuminated by a candle, and decorated with some fir branches. Suddenly, outside my cell, I heard my number called. Usually that did not mean anything good. It meant interrogations or punishment. I rose and followed the guard who led me downstairs from my cell in the third storey. We entered another cell. "Bring number 212 to this cell also"; he barked to another guard. Eventually the heavy cell door swung open and another prisoner was brought in. "You asked for a clergyman. Here is Dr. Lilje" '.

Immediately I knew what was expected of me. The prisoner was to die and he had asked for prayers and for Communion. I was more than ready to do what was asked. Another prisoner was summoned – a violinist who I knew was under sentence of death – so there were four of us in the cell. The violinist played a chorale. I read the gospel for Christmas day:

'Now it came to pass in those days that there went out a decree . . .'
'I prayed aloud the beautiful old prayer of confession of St. Thomas à Kempis, and then pronounced absolution. It was a very quiet celebration of the Sacrament, full of deep confidence in God. We were prisoners in the power of the Gestapo in Berlin but the peace of God enfolded us: it was real and present, like a Hand laid gently upon us'.

2. *Desmond Tutu tells of Communion in a South African street*
'I visited one of these banned people, Winnie Mandela. Her husband is serving a life sentence on Robben Island, our maximum security prison. I wanted to take her Holy Communion. The police told me I couldn't enter her house. So we celebrated Holy Communion in my car in the street, in Christian South Africa. On a second occasion I went to see her on a weekend. Her restriction order was more strict at weekends. She couldn't leave her yard. So we celebrated Holy Communion again in the street. This time Winnie was on one side of the fence and I on the other.'

3. *Communion on the moon*
'On the day of the moon landing we awoke at 5.30 a.m., Houston time. Neil and I separated from Mike Collins in the command module. Our powered descent was right on schedule. With only seconds worth of fuel left, we touched down at 3.30 p.m., . . . Now was the time for Communion.

So I unstowed the elements in their flight packets. I put them and the Scripture reading on the little table in front of the abort guidance-system computer. Then I called "Houston, this is Eagle. This is LM Pilot speaking. I would like to request a few moments silence. I would like to invite each person listening in, wherever and whomever he may be, to contemplate for a moment the events of the past few hours and to give thanks in his own individual way."

For me, this meant taking Communion. In the blackout I opened the little plastic packages which contained bread and wine. I poured wine into the chalice my parish had given me. In the one-sixth gravity of the moon, the wine curled slowly and gracefully up the cup. It was interesting to think that the very first liquid ever poured on the moon, and the first food eaten there, were consecrated elements.

Just before I partook of the elements, I read the words which I had chosen to indicate our trust that as man probes into space, we are in fact acting in Christ. I sensed especially strong my unity with our church back home, and with the Church everywhere.

I read: " 'I am the vine, you are the branches. Whoever remains in me, and I in him, will bear much fruit; for you can do nothing without me." '

Buzz Aldrin, one of the first astronauts on the moon

Hymn

The introductory line to each verse should be spoken by the leader.

Let's sing with thanksgiving about our tables at home.

1. Each family
   At table meets;
   From home and school
   Each other greet:
   A time to talk,
   A time to eat,
   Welcome and love
   Each day repeat.

Let's sing with sorrow and hope about the tables across the world.

2. Some tables full;
   Some sadly bare:
   To sacrifice
   Who now will dare?
   Then, giving thanks,
   Begin to share,
   Since Christ the Lord
   Invites our care.

Let's sing in anticipation of the table in church.

3. We gather round
   A table here.
   We meet as friends,
   The Lord is near.
   With bread and wine
   We celebrate:
   By sign and word
   Christ's love relate.

(The tune can be found on page 36)   Donald Hilton

Dramatic reading

Three people dressed in first century costume move to the front of the church, speaking as they walk. They are three of the first disciples though, apart from Matthew, they do not need to be identified.

ONE   There are some days that just stay in your memory for ever.

Two	So many of the days we spent with Jesus were like that – unforgettable!
One	That day by the sea-side at Galilee. We'd seen him before, heard him speak. But the way he looked at us! It was as though he saw deep into my life and soul. 'Follow me!', he said. I could have run a mile, yet I could do nothing but stand there knowing that my life was going to be different from that moment.
Matthew	I was just doing my job, sitting at the tax desk like I always did, day after dreary day. To tell the truth I was thinking about him. I'd heard him speak the day before and couldn't get him out of my mind. He used the same words to me. 'Follow me', he said. I'd have gone a hundred miles with him, wherever he wanted.
Two	We did! More than a hundred! Not always willingly, and certainly not always with understanding. But we went. Couldn't do much else, really. Not if life was to have any meaning.
One	Do you remember when they tried to trap him about paying the temple tax?
Two	. . . and when that boy gave the loaves and fishes?
One	. . . and that young lad possessed by demons (devils)? I felt so sorry for him
Two	. . . especially as it came just after that time on the mountain, That was a day I'll never forget. Never.
One	And all those stories he told that made his teaching come alive for us. Remember them? What about you, Matthew? What's going through your mind?
Matthew	It's the final week that sticks in my mind, and especially the last few days. All those plans we never fully understood. Donkeys and passwords, palms waving in the air, and children shouting . Then later still, walking through the streets to that room he'd got ready for us. Up the stairs we went and sat together whilst he talked to us.
Two	If only we had known what was to happen in the next few days!
One	Perhaps it was a good job we didn't.
Two	We'd had so many meals with him, but that was special. It was Passover, of course, but more than that. It was as though something very old and precious was being turned into something new.

ONE	And even more precious.

> *While they speak Matthew moves to a table where paper and a quill pen are set out. As the others stop talking he begins to write, speaking as he does so. The actor should speak slowly and in phrases as someone does who reads whilst writing.*

MATTHEW During supper Jesus took bread, and having said the blessing he broke it and gave it to the disciples with the words: 'Take this and eat; this is my body.' Then he took a cup, and having offered thanks to God he gave it to them with the words: 'Drink from it, all of you. For this is my blood, the blood of the covenant, shed for many for the forgiveness of sins. I tell you, never again shall I drink from this fruit of the vine until that day when I drink it new with you in the kingdom of my Father.'

Matthew 26.26-29 (REB)

> *As Matthew finishes and the three move away several people of mixed ages move forward and prepare the communion table with a cloth, bread and wine. Use one large loaf which can later be passed around for all to receive a piece. Let the table be prepared either in silence or with soft music. As those preparing the table complete their task the leader speaks.*

Leader
Come, for all things are now ready. The memory of the Church is your memory. Come and share with Matthew, Peter, John, Mary and Martha, with Clare and Francis, with Benedict, Teresa, Luther and Wesley, and with all others throughout the world who, on this Sunday morning, find refreshment and renewal as they live within and further the rich memory of the people of God

Prayer of Thanksgiving
In the name of the Lord Jesus Christ, we give thanks to you, our God.
You have travelled with your people, before them and behind, to left and right. The long years are testimony to your love. The Church rejoices in your gift of faith. The unseen multitudes are our sisters and brothers. The chorus of praise echoes down the centuries, and speeds its way into the future. Little children sing of your goodness, and the voice of old age replies with joy.

21

And now, at your invitation we sit at the table to which Christ has welcomed his people. The bread will remind us that the body of Christ was broken to mend our shattered lives. The wine will tell its story of Christ, whose love was so strong that he was ready to suffer for his friends. And he calls us his friends. Thanks be to you, our God, for ever. Amen

Other Communion prayers of thanksgiving may also be used.

Breaking of bread. *Let each share the one loaf.*

Sharing the wine *Let each drink from the cup or cups.*

Prayer of dedication
Father, as we recall those many people who through the long years have helped us to be Christians and pointed us to the life of faith so may we encourage others. Help us to be generous and loving, faithful and gracious so that in years to come we may ourselves be remembered as those who witnessed to Christ and lived in his way. Amen

Hymn   'Now let us from this table rise'
              or 'Brother, Sister, let me serve you'
              or 'We come unto our faithful (father's) God'
                  (First and last verse)

Benediction

LET'S CELEBRATE WITH A FEAST!

Introduction

Most of our meals are planned for the simple reason that we are hungry. The rushed breakfast before leaving for work or the snatched sandwich before a meeting are hardly celebrations. The meals we remember, however, are those that carry an additional significance – the birthday tea, the candle-lit wedding anniversary meal, the wedding breakfast, or the church anniversary tea. These occasions are invested with a significance far beyond the need to satisfy our hunger.

The communion services of the early church probably served both purposes. They were normal meals for hungry people but they were also a commemoration of the Last Supper. It may well be that they began with a full meal and then moved on to a symbolic meal of remembrance and celebration. This would explain Paul's criticism (*1 Corinthians 11.17ff*) of those who destroyed the meaning of the sacramental element by a lack of sharing and true fellowship in the earlier full meal.

This festival service seeks to retain the link between 'normal' eating and 'sacramental' eating. If the service is planned for the usual Sunday morning time this can be done with a brief party or a vivid reminder of earlier parties, anniversary meals etc., followed by the communion service. The service would have greater significance, however, if it was planned for a special occasion – an anniversary or church family day – when a lunch or tea could be provided, followed by the communion meal. What is offered on the following pages will need to be adjusted in the light of local plans and possibilities. Towards the end of the service the opportunity is given for people – who have just shared in a feast – to give a party to others.

Preparation

Decide how the 'party' element is to be introduced e.g. if it is a midday lunch or later afternoon tea there will be catering to be organised. If the service has to be the usual late-morning, say

23

10.45 a.m., a simple breakfast party might be held in the quarter of an hour before the service or as the service begins. Details for these possibilities are given in the **Order of Service** itself.

In all cases both an iced party-cake and a loaf for communion have to be made. Invite two different families in the church to do this.

Decide how the story of the prodigal son is to be presented and make the necessary plans e.g., organise the acting or prepare the posters.

Decide for which group of people outside your local church community you are going to prepare the later party. Fix the date, venue etc. in advance so that a clear request can be made within the service for people to assist. Help them to see this, not as a postscript to the service but as the service continuing into everyday life.

ORDER OF SERVICE

Begin the act of worship with a party
If the time of service allows let this be a midday meal or afternoon tea. Introduce aspects that all ages will recognise as celebratory. For example, if the event is near to Christmas use streamers and crackers etc. If it is a church anniversary then ask a group to prepare paper hats for everyone marked with 'Happy Birthday!' or the age of the church: '295 today!' For a service near to Pentecost plan red paper hats with a flame of fire, or dove on them. A service on Easter Day might be preceded by breakfast.

If the service is held on a normal Sunday at, say 10.45 a.m., then the party will have to be symbolic and brief. Tea, coffee, soft drinks and biscuits can be offered. Paper hats, party poppers, and streamers can still be used.

Call to worship
On this mountain the Lord of Hosts will prepare a banquet of rich fare for all the peoples, a banquet of wines well-matured, richest fare and well-matured wines strained clear.
On that day the people will say: 'See this is our God; we have waited for him and he will deliver us. This is the Lord for whom we have waited; let us rejoice and exult in his deliverance.'

Isaiah 25.6-7, 9 (REB)

Hymn   A hymn of celebration e.g.
             'New songs of celebration render'
             or 'Sing, one and all, a song of celebration'

Prayer

Sunday is celebration day:
>the first day of creation;
>the day of Jesus' triumph;
>the day of the gift of the Holy Spirit;
>the first day of a new week.

Lord, help us to celebrate this Sunday;
>to rejoice in the gifts of your creation;
>to find new life in Jesus and his gifts;
>to set our sights on your way for the week ahead;
>to enjoy being in your church in fellowship and worship.

Thank you, God, for this celebration day

from Prayers for the Church Community

Reading   Luke 15.11-31

Prepare the story dramatically. Any of the following suggestions might be used:

- *Illustrate the story with picture-posters prepared in advance.*
- *Act out the story as it is being read.*
- *Plan for people (different ages, of course) to walk across the front of the church as the story is read and hold up placards with short newspaper-type headlines e.g., 'son demands cash', 'local family divided over inheritance', 'reckless living rewarded', 'local family united again' 'party to beat all parties', 'father's love sticks'.*

Prayer

Father, the story comes home to us. It is our own story.
We are the younger son:
>we have grabbed at life,
>demanded our dues,
>and worshipped pleasure.

We are the older son:
>we have been jealous of kindness given to others,
>we have crowded out the forgiving spirit,
>and resented good fortune that came to others.

May we become like the father:
>welcoming and loving,
>forgiving and celebrating,

Like God.

25

Hymn   'God is love: let heaven adore him'
           or other hymn to declare God's forgiving love

Party-time
If the service did not begin with a party plan a simple, short celebration at this point in the service. Serve soft drinks and biscuits. Quickly hang up streamers. Use party poppers. Play cheerful music. Then show the iced party-cake and divide it so that everyone has a piece. If the party has already been held share the cake immediately.

Readings
Whilst the cake is being distributed and eaten read some of the following. Remind the congregation of the old monastic custom of reading spiritual literature during a meal. The purpose of these readings is to move people's thoughts towards the Lord's table and the communion.

1. An intriguing thing happened when BBC TV's first 'Global Report' documentary was being filmed. One of the programmed opening shots was of a hundred people representing the human family, standing together on a grassy slope. The hundred had been selected by nationality so there were a lot of Chinese and not many Swedes. Everyone wore national costume and brought representative lunches: the small group of Americans had before them a sumptuous, meat-filled picnic, while the larger group of Indians beside them looked sadly on their meagre portions of boiled rice.
    What happened? Spontaneous sharing. The Americans invited the Indians over: the response was natural and seemed inevitable. No explanations, no haranguing – because the sense of community was there, of being one family. Can what works in microcosm work in macrocosm?

    New Internationalist

2. In a film report from Ethiopia Michael Buerk from the BBC wrote:
    We were in a town filming and we hadn't anything to eat. Somebody told us where we could get something. If you've got money there is food you can buy.
    So we went to this place and had a Coco Cola and a little bread roll each. We were just about to start eating when in the doorway there must have been about fifty or sixty people. You

know, children looking with big, wide eyes, an old man who fell
on his knees and came shuffling into the cafe, and started kissing
my feet. The very idea of actually eating that bread roll, I mean, I
would have been sick on the spot.

Instinctively, you start breaking the bread into tiny little
pieces, which isn't going to help anybody, and start giving to
people – and hundreds more come clustering round the doorway.

3. John 6.3-11

Prayer of intercession
Father and God,
even the silent hills shout aloud to celebrate your goodness,
the depths of the ocean are high in your praise,
stars dance and shine in widening circles of light,
and the sun and the moon smile at each other.

And we are with them in their joy, Father and God
Every day is celebration day:
life flows, joy rings out, men and women are touched by delight,
spring bursts into summer, flows to its fullness in autumn
splendour, and runs its full term in winter's cleansing cold.
How do you do it, Father and God:
    to bring your people such delight?

And yet a shadow falls across our joy
and dims the brightness of our light.
For some the party is over, or never began.
Sadness and grief knock on lonely doors,
the once warm welcome of a joyful home feels icy blasts.
The well remembered satisfaction of a job well done is framed in
    wasteful unemployment,
and childhood's innocent delight is tarnished with abuse and
    shame.

Father still, and still our God
receive our joy and hear our pain,
Still we must celebrate your wondrous gifts
    and call you close to bear with us
    the anguish of a tragic world,
    through Jesus Christ our Lord. Amen

Hymn   'Jesus the Lord says, I am the bread'
              or 'The kingdom of God is justice and joy'

The institution of the Lord's Supper: 1 Corinthians 11.23-26

Prayer of thanksgiving
    We give you thanks, O Father, for the life and knowledge which
    you have made known to us through your son Jesus; yours is the
    glory for ever and ever. As this bread was scattered upon the
    mountains, and being gathered together became one, so may
    your Church be gathered together from the ends of the earth into
    your kingdom; for yours is the glory and the power, through
    Jesus Christ, for ever and ever. Amen
                                                    from the *Didache, 2nd Century*

Breaking and sharing of the bread
Instead of the usual music whilst the bread is distributed use any of the
remaining spiritual readings given earlier in the service, or read
John 21.4-12a (ending 'Come and have breakfast').

Sharing of the wine
When the wine has been shared announce that the church is to organise a
party for a group of people who do not always share in the joy and gaiety of
life. We'll spread our party celebration to others. Give the date, time and
other brief details and invite people who want to help to give their names to
stewards at the door as they go out. In this way the 'party for the party-less'
will be seen to be a direct response to the joy of the church's celebration.

Prayer
    Since we have so much to celebrate, eternal God, give us the
    opportunity to lift the spirits of others and draw them into the
    circle of our happiness. Amen

Hymn   'Now let us from this table rise'

Benediction

BROKEN TO MEND

Introduction

The Communion Service is celebrated by a reconciled and reconciling community. Women and men, children and older people, people with different jobs, or no job, those with different backgrounds, histories and futures meet at the table; symbol and sign of the new community that Jesus has created.

It is not a community that we could make ourselves. We are broken people living in a fractured world. Jesus mends our brokenness. We see this powerfully expressed as he, the Lord, stoops to wash his disciples feet, and even more powerfully in his dying on the Cross.

The service is based around three litanies. The first recognises our brokenness, the second that in Christ we have been accepted and so form a new community, and the third, coming at the end of the service, is a litany of commitment that takes us out into God's world to do His work. The Lord's Supper is shared between the second and third litanies. Fed at the table the whole community is ready to serve others.

Preparation

Reproduce the litanies so that each member of the congregation has a copy. Rehearse the litanies with a small group so that a clear lead is given to the congregation. Choose people to read the call to worship. Prepare the dance sequence. Select music. Choose the activity that will express the theme of belonging and make preparations accordingly.

ORDER OF SERVICE

Call to worship   *Use at least two voices.*
Isaiah offers a vision of a world renewed by God:
> See, I am creating new heavens and a new earth!
> The past will be no more remembered nor will it ever come to mind.

Rejoice and be for ever filled with delight at what I create;
  for I am creating Jerusalem as a delight and her people as a
  joy.
I shall take delight in Jerusalem and rejoice in my people;
  the sound of weeping, the cry of distress
  will be heard in her no more.
No child will ever again die in infancy,
  no old man fail to live out his span of life.
He who dies at a hundred is just a youth,
  if he does not attain a hundred he is thought accursed!
My people will build houses and live in them,
  plant vineyards and eat their fruit;
  they will not build for others to live in or plant for others to
  eat.
They will be as long-lived as a tree,
  and my chosen ones will enjoy the fruit of their labour.
They will not toil to no purpose or raise children for misfortune,
  because they and their issues after them
  are a race blessed by the Lord.
Even before they call to me, I shall answer,
  and while they are still speaking I shall respond.
The wolf and the lamb will feed together
  and the lion will eat straw like the ox,
  and as for the serpent its food will be dust.
Neither hurt not harm will be done in all my holy mountain,
  says the Lord

Isaiah 65.17-25 (REB)

Hymn
Choose a hymn that acknowledges human brokenness and fault.
    e.g., 'Praise to the Holiest in the height'

A Litany of Confession
Invite the congregation to use the response.
    Eternal God, you made the world a splendid place,
        beautiful in all its forms,
        ordered and complete.
    But we are greedy people and selfish, and we have spoiled your
    good creation.

Response   **Come, Lord, mend our brokenness;**
            restore the earth to what you first intended.

Eternal God, you gave us food and drink enough for all,
   the air was fresh and clear,
      deep running rivers fed the wide oceans in purity,
      green were the plants for food, and bright the growing
      flowers.
But we are greedy people and selfish, and failed to share your
gifts.

Response   **Come, Lord, mend our brokenness;**
               restore the earth to what you first intended.

Eternal God, you wanted everyone to be happy,
   you intended people to live together in peace,
   you made us able to love so that no-one would be lonely,
But we are greedy people and selfish, and we have spoiled our
own lives and those of others.

Response   **Come, Lord, mend our brokenness;**
               show us how to live the way you first intended.

Eternal God, you made us different: black and brown and white,
   you gave us land and nations, room enough for all to live,
   you made men and women, boys and girls, little children,
   grown-up people to live together in harmony,
      one but many; many but one.
But we are greedy selfish people and we have turned our
differences into reasons for war and argument, spoiling our own
lives and that those of others.

Response   **Come, Lord, mend our brokenness;**
               show us how to live the way you first intended.

Eternal God, you gave us a Church: splendid variety, unity in
faith,
   you taught us how to pray in different forms,
   colour and simplicity, silence and speaking feed our worship,
   friends of Jesus, you gave us friendship for each other.
But we are thoughtless selfish people. We thought that
everyone should be like us. We have spoiled our Christian
friendship.

Response   **Come, Lord, mend our brokenness;**
               show us how to live the way you first intended.

31

A period of silent reflection with music.
We are thoughtless selfish people.

Response   **Come, Lord, mend our brokenness;**
                 show us how to live the way you first intended.

Hymn   'Lord, Jesus Christ, you have come to us'

Reading   Romans 5.6–11

Dance sequence
A group of dancers express the experience of brokenness and then community.

A Litany of Acceptance
Invite the congregation to use the responses.
Lord, when we were outside you called us in,
lost in a foreign country you were our passport to a new life,
across a chasm you built us a bridge,
imprisoned, you made the walls come tumbling down.

Response   **Accepting God,**
                 our sins and foolishness forgiven,
                 we live secure in your love.

Lord, when sin had driven us away, you spoke a forgiving word,
aliens through shame, you welcomed us back,
when we didn't even like ourselves, you said you loved us.

Response   **Accepting God,**
                 our sins and foolishness forgiven,
                 we live secure in your love.

Lord, selfishness cornered us but you drew us back into the circle,
friendship gone, you opened your loving arms to us,
walking a lonely road, we found you by our side.

Response   **Accepting God,**
                 our sins and foolishness forgiven,
                 we live secure in your love.

Lord once we were nothing and you made us something,
once cut off, you united us,
once nameless and forgotten, you remembered us,
and gave a us new name.

Response **Accepting God,**
our sins and foolishness forgiven,
we live secure in your love.

A period of silent reflection with music.
Lord you have given us a new name.

Response **Accepting God,**
our sins and foolishness forgiven,
we live secure in your love.

Comment

The world is a broken place. So many of our national and
international problems are of our own making. Nations are greedy
for the land and resources of others. Prejudice makes us dislike
people we have never even met. The variety of human colours,
traditions, cultures, and life-styles, which God gave us out of his rich
imagination we have made into barriers, and walls. We worship
death.

It would be understandable if God turned his back and had
nothing more to do with us. We've spoiled his creation. We've
marred the humanity he gave us. We have taken friendship and
turned it into enmity.

Humpty Dumpty sat on a wall,
Humpty Dumpty had a great fall,
All the king's horses and all the king's men,
Couldn't put Humpty together again.

That's the world we've made. We've fallen off our wall. We've broken
ourselves and nobody can put us together again. All alike have
sinned , and are deprived of the divine glory.

Romans 3.23 (REB)

And Paul gives the answer to our dilemma. 'Who is there to rescue
me from this state of death?' 'Who but God? Thanks be to him
through Jesus Christ our Lord!'

Romans 7.25 (REB)

God in Christ has mended us when we were broken. His action is the cross. By being broken himself, Christ has mended us. By dying, he has given us life. When we take bread and break it we are reminded that the Humpty Dumpty broken world has gone for us.

What kind of people meet at the Lord's table? We are people who know we have done wrong, but know just as deeply that God has forgiven us. He has washed our feet – so now we are free to serve others.

Reading   John 13.3–17 *This is used as the Institution of the Supper.*

We belong together
Express the unity of the local church in some visible way. For example: hold hands around the congregation whilst music is played.

Toss balls of wool around the congregation, the wool-strand being retained by some whilst the ball is thrown further so that eventually the whole congregation is intertwined.

Invite each member of the congregation to write their name on a strip of coloured paper approximately 18cm x 3cm. Then link the strips in a chain, using a stapler so that they hang together. Commercial garland paper can be used.

Hymn   'The church is like a table'
            or 'Bind us together, Lord'

Prayers of thanksgiving
(Use traditional prayers from a service book)

The breaking of bread

The sharing of bread and wine

A Litany of Commitment
Invite the congregation to use the response.

> Father, because you have loved us, we have strength to love others.

> **Response**   **In shop and street, at home, away,
> in school and park, in work and rest,
> we will tell of your greatness
> and serve those who need us.**

Lord Jesus Christ, you washed the feet of your friends
Prompted by love, you suffered and died

Response   In shop and street . . .

Holy Spirit of God,
out of chaos you brought order, into darkness you brought light.
You are renewing the face of the earth
and you are making us into new people.

Response   In shop and street . . .

A period of silent reflection with music.
Father, you love us.
Lord Jesus Christ, you serve us.
Holy Spirit, you turn us into new people

Response   In shop and street . . .

Hymn   'Now let us from this table rise'
or 'For the healing of the nations'

Affirmation
See, I am creating new heavens and a new earth!
The past will be no more remembered nor will it ever come to
mind.
Rejoice and be for ever filled with delight at what I create;
For I am creating Jerusalem as a delight and her people as a
joy.

Isaiah 65.17-18 (REB)

Benediction

DE LUFFA

Colin Peters

Intro, and between verses

COMMUNION   Colin Peters

Flowing
Intro. and between verses

ACKNOWLEDGEMENTS

The editor and publishers gratefully acknowledge permission to reproduce the following copyright material.

Every effort has been made to trace copyright owners but if any rights have been inadvertently overlooked, the necessary correction will be made in subsequent editions. We apologise for any apparent negligence.

Michel Quoist:
>   Adapted from *Prayers of Life*, used by permission of Gill & Son.

Iona Community:
>   *In the beginning God made the world*, from *Liturgy of Life* (NCEC), for which permission was sought.

C.H. Dodd:
>   From *The Founder of Christianity*, used by permission of Collins.

Dom Gregory Dix:
>   From *The Shape of the Liturgy*, used by permission of A & C Black.

We are grateful to quote from the following version of the Bible:
REB   The *Revised English Bible* (© 1989 Oxford and Cambridge University Presses).

A Collection Of Collections

LITURGY OF LIFE

Compiled by Donald Hilton.
In corporate acts of worship in all the mainstream churches the same basic elements can be seen. This anthology broadly follows the liturgy of the Churches bringing into the sanctuary the everyday experiences and thoughts which interlock with the main components of Christian worship.

Liturgy of Life is intended both to aid personal devotion and reflection, and also to provide material for Christian education and worship.

A WORD IN SEASON

Compiled by Donald Hilton.
This anthology is a collection of material designed to be used in Christian education and worship in churches and schools. The sequence follows the pattern of the year beginning with Advent. Overtly Christian items are mixed with material from other sources.

TURN BUT A STONE

By Edmund Banyard
This new collection of prayers and meditations written by Edmund Banyard is intended as a stimulation to thought, both for personal devotion and as an aid in corporate worship. It expands on the themes of the Bible readings suggested in the *Joint Liturgical Group Lectionary (JLG2)*. Edmund's earlier book *Word Alive*, an anthology of works from around the world, was used as a companion to the previous lectionary (JLG1).

REFLECTIONS

By Cyril Franks.
The Gospels speak to us today and every day. In this collection of thirty-one readings from St Matthew's Gospel we are invited to draw nearer to Christ as we reflect on Matthew's writings in our daily lives. Each passage is accompanied by a thought-provoking meditation.

MORE RESOURCES FOR ALL AGE WORSHIP FROM NCEC

CELEBRATING SERIES

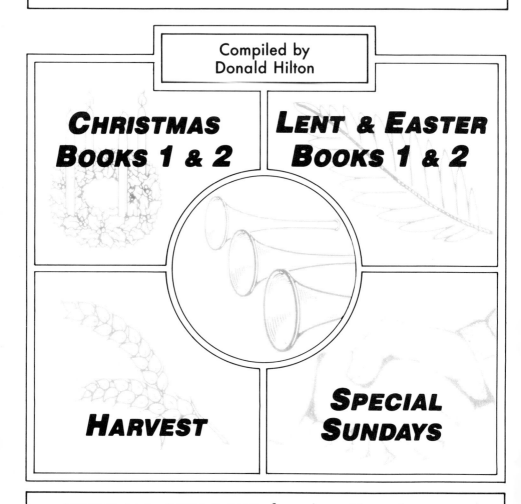

Compiled by
Donald Hilton

CHRISTMAS BOOKS 1 & 2

LENT & EASTER BOOKS 1 & 2

HARVEST

SPECIAL SUNDAYS

FESTIVAL SERVICES for the Church Year

Sold individually or in a set with a substantial saving

Available from all good Christian bookshops or, in case of difficulty, from NCEC direct.